Art Fraud

Jeffrey Schrader

BlazeVOX [books]

Buffalo, New York

Art Fraud by Jeffrey Schrader

First Edition
ISBN: 9781935402787
Library of Congress Control Number 9781935402787

BlazeVOX [books]
303 Bedford Ave
Buffalo, NY 14216

Editor@blazevox.org

publisher of weird little books

BlazeVOX [books]

blazevox.org

2   4   6   8   0   9   7   5   3   1

B   X

Art Fraud

Would you state your full name for the record?

Publisher

Where do you presently reside?

California.

Are you presently employed?

Yes.

What is your present employment?

Publishing.

And who is your employer?

Myself.

Is the company incorporated, to your knowledge?

No, it isn't.

Is that a dba for you?

Yes.

Has that been true since its founding?

Yes.

What are the responsibilities of General Manager at Publishing House?

General manager.

Do those responsibilities include any editorial responsibilities?

Not really.

Who within Publishing House is the employee or employees that had editing responsibilities over the past four years for the publications of Publishing House?

Did you say editing?

Yes, sir.

Objection in that there is no foundation laid that he would know that.

You're the publisher of Publishing House, correct?

Yes.

Is that the most senior position within that company?

Yes.

Who reports to you as publisher of Publishing House? What employees report to you?

Everybody else.

And how many employees does Publishing House have?

About seventy.

Seventy. Who is the next most senior employee within Publishing House?

Senior Editor

And what is Senior Editor's title?

Publisher.

Same as yours?

Yes. Well, she's vice president and publisher.

And you are president and publisher?

Yeah.

How many - - do you know how many employees your company employs that have any editing responsibility?

I don't know.

Can you give me an estimate?

Ten or fifteen.

Do your responsibilities include any editing responsibilities?

Yes.

Would that also be true for Senior Editor?

Yes.

What about General Manager?

Limited.

Does Publishing House, or has Publishing House over the course of the past four years, to your knowledge, had any policy as to checking books that it's publishing for accuracy?

Yes.

And what is that policy?

We look carefully at each book.

And what do you look for?

Errors of any kind.

All right. Let's be specific. Do you recall your company publishing <u>Art</u> by a woman named Gallery Owner?

Yes.

Is <u>Art</u> in more than one edition?

Yes.

In the production of documents by your company, there were no copies of any manuscripts or any marked up copies of those, of any publications by Gallery Owner. Are you aware of whether or not in the company's files there are such manuscripts?

I don't know.

Do you know what the practice of your company would be as to a book that it's published, with regard to marked-up copies of manuscripts?

Oftentimes they are thrown away, oftentimes they are sent back to the authors.

Are they sometimes kept in the company?

Yes.

Do you know how many books of Gallery Owner's your company has published?

Yes.

How many?

Three.

Can you give me the names of those books?

<u>Art</u>. <u>Art</u>, second edition. <u>Art</u>, third edition.

When was the second edition of <u>Art</u> published?

I don't know the publication date.

Has it been recent?

Sort of.

Who within your company would know?

Senior Editor would know.

What involvement if any did you have in the publication of the first edition of <u>Art</u>?

A specific question?

That is the specific question. What involvement if any did you have in the publication of that first edition of <u>Art</u>?

A fair amount.

Why don't you describe for me what role you played in the publication of that book?

Objection as to time. What period of time are we talking about?

Any period of time.

Overbroad.

I contracted with Gallery Owner. I reviewed the pictures, and I selected the designer. That was mainly what I did.

Did you review in any way the text of <u>Art</u>?

Not really.

In reviewing the pictures, by that do you mean the photographs of artwork that were included in the book?

Yes.

What did you do in reviewing those pictures?

Helped select.

I'm sorry, helped select what?

The pictures.

What pictures would be included in the book?

Yes.

What criteria did you use in guiding you in helping to select which pictures would be included in the book?

The ones that were the most interesting.

Visually interesting?

Yes.

In the work you did on selecting the pictures that were included in the book, did you consult with Gallery Owner in making those selections?

No, not really.

Did you consult with anyone else in making - -

Yes.

- - those selections? Who else did you consult with?

Designer.

And who is Designer?

He's an outside consultant.

Do you know if he had a company that he does consulting through, or was it just under his own name?

Own name.

Do you know where he is today?

No, I don't.

Did you consult with anyone else other than Designer in your selection of which pictures to include in <u>Art</u>?

No.

Do you know what criteria if any Designer used in consulting with you on which pictures should be included?

We wanted the most interesting pictures.

And again, just so I'm clear, by "interesting" do you mean anything other than the visual appearance of the picture?

"Most interesting" covers the ground.

What ground?

The extent of our interest in our selecting process.

Did you, in the selecting process, then, include knowledge about the history of any of these pictures?

We didn't write any text.

I understand that. When you say "interesting covers the ground," I'm trying to understand what was of interest to you or to Designer.

Color, size, form, condition.

Anything else?

Fame. Some are more famous.

Anything else?

Their historical position in Artist's work.

Anything else?

No.

Do you recall if you or Designer made any efforts during the selection process to determine whether any of the pictures selected for <u>Art</u> were photographs of fakes, artwork that was in fact not by Artist?

Never occurred to us.

The pictures that you and Designer reviewed in this selection process for <u>Art</u>, who supplied those pictures to you?

Gallery Owner.

And that's true in every instance?

Yes.

Did you ever discuss with Gallery Owner whether or not she had any concerns that any of the pictures she was supplying you were photographs of fakes, works of art that were not in fact done by Artist?

No.

It never came up?

No.

Is it correct that your company has published art books involving other artists?

Yes.

Were you involved in the selection process for the pictures that were included in any of those art books?

Yes.

All of them?

No.

For the ones that you were involved in, did the question ever arise as to whether or not any of the pictures being reviewed for publication might be pictures of fakes?

Never. Never was a question.

So in your experience as a publisher, right up until the publication of <u>Art</u> is it fair to say that to your knowledge the question of fakes being included in any book published by your company had never arisen?

Right.

Between the publication of <u>Art</u> and <u>Art</u>, second edition, did you come to understand that there was an assertion that some of the works pictured in <u>Art</u> were in fact fakes?

Yes.

How did you first learn about this?

I don't remember.

Do you remember who first told you about that?

I don't remember.

Do you remember if you formed an opinion as to whether or not any of the works depicted in <u>Art</u> were fakes?

Yes.

And what opinion did you form?

I didn't think there were any fakes.

What was the basis for that opinion?

Just an opinion.

Did you speak with anyone in arriving at that opinion?

No.

Did you review any documents in arriving at that opinion?

I read a letter from someone, I think, that asserted that there were a couple of fakes, or a few fakes. And it didn't appear accurate to me.

Why didn't it appear accurate to you?

Just didn't.

You don't recall any reason for believing that?

Didn't appear accurate.

You don't recall why?

No.

Other than Gallery Owner, have you ever spoken to any other individuals who purported to be knowledgeable about the work of Artist, regarding the pictures contained in <u>Art</u>?

Yes.

Who?

Art Writer.

Anyone else?

Art Critic.

Anyone else?

I don't recall any others right now.

What discussions do you recall having with Art Writer regarding the issue of whether or not any of the works pictured in <u>Art</u> were fakes?

Can I have a specific question?

That is a specific question, sir. Do you need it read back?

I need it again.

What discussions do you recall having with Art Writer regarding the issue of whether or not any of the works pictured in <u>Art</u> were fakes?

Discussions 1 and 2.

Tell me about discussion 1.

He visited my office, we had a discussion. He called me on the phone, we had another discussion.

When he visited your office, what did he say to you?

I don't remember.

What did you say to him?

I don't remember.

Do you remember telling him that you didn't care whether or not there were fakes pictured in <u>Art</u>?

No.

Do you remember telling him that in the phone conversation?

No.

Is it your testimony that you didn't tell him that?

No.

You don't remember one way or the other whether you told him that?

Right.

Did you, as president of Publishing House, ever formulate an opinion as to whether or not you were concerned that <u>Art</u> might be depicting fake works of art?

It was never a concern.

Why was it never a concern?

Because, first, I wasn't aware that there were any fakes in the book. I never received any information from anybody that convinced me that there were fakes. And the book got exceedingly good reviews in the art world. Never any mention of any fakes.

Isn't it correct that you were aware that Art Writer and Art Critic asserted that the book contained fakes?

At some point I was. I think they asserted that, yes.

Did you ever become aware that Boston Art Gallery also asserted that there were fakes included in <u>Art</u>?

I don't remember that.

Objection. No foundation.

Did you ever become aware that New York City Art Gallery asserted that there were fakes in <u>Art</u>?

I've never heard of that gallery.

Did anyone other than Gallery Owner ever give you an opinion that there were no fakes included in <u>Art</u>?

Objection. No foundation that Gallery Owner told him that.

You can answer, if you understand the question.

Repeat the question.

Well, let's break it down so I can deal with counsel's objections. Did Gallery Owner ever tell you that there were no fakes included in <u>Art</u>?

No.

Did you ever ask her?

No.

Did you ever, as a publisher, feel you had a duty to investigate whether or not there were any fakes included in <u>Art</u>?

No.

Why not?

That wasn't my part of the process.

Whose part of the process was it?

Objection. Assumes that it's someone's part of the process.

You can answer the question.

I relied on the author.

Gallery Owner?

Yes.

Is it correct that as a publisher you believed as long as you were relying on the author, you had no duty to further investigate whether any fakes were included in <u>Art</u>?

Duty?

Yes, sir.

How would you describe "duty" in this case?

Why don't you give me your definition of duty?

Counsel - -

I just want to reach - -

- - this deponent is not here to provide you with - -

Counsel, this is a time-honored way of dealing with a witness's confusion about a word.

If you want to phrase a question - -

I'm going to. Are you instructing this witness not to answer?

No, I'm not. I'm telling you that there are ways to communicate effectively, and one of them is to ask clear questions. You're using terms of art about duty, and asking him to give definitions. If you would like to ask a clear question, I'm sure that he would be happy to answer it.

Thank you, Counsel. I look forward to your seminar on depositions. The question is this, sir. What is your definition of the word "duty"? Not mine. Yours.

It assumes that you have one. Answer the question if you have a definition of duty.

I don't have a definition of duty.

No definition at all? All right. Let's try the word "responsibility." Do you have a definition of that?

Publishers have the responsibility to not publish fiction as nonfiction - - if they want to.

Do you believe that as part of that responsibility, Publishing House had any responsibility to ensure that the supposedly nonfiction <u>Art</u> didn't include any fakes?

Objection. This is beyond the scope of this deposition. It's irrelevant, it's harassing, and the tone of voice is very disrespectful. I would admonish counsel to treat this deponent respectfully with a tone of voice worthy of courtesy.

Let the record reflect I have.

You can answer the question, sir.

Would you repeat the question?

Sure. Does your sense of Publishing House's responsibility, that you just described, include a responsibility that it not publish <u>Art</u> with fakes in it?

My duty was to publish an excellent book that would get good reviews, that would be reviewed by the art world, the art media, the art critics, and be favorably received.

And that was the extent of your - -

That all happened.

And that was the extent of your duty as you understood it?

That's what I tried to do.

So basically you didn't care whether <u>Art</u> included any fakes in it, did you?

It was never a question.

You're being very argumentative with this deponent, Counsel.

How about <u>Art</u>, second edition, was there ever a question that that book included any fakes?

There was a question after the first edition. And we put a disclaimer in the book saying that there was a controversy about some of the works that we included.

And if you had been aware of that controversy before the publication of the first edition, would you have included the same disclaimer?

Objection. Calls for speculation.

I don't know.

How did you come to learn that there was a controversy about the authenticity of some of the works that were included in <u>Art</u>?

I don't specifically remember.

Did you ever discuss the issue with Gallery Owner?

I think so.

And what do you recall of those discussions?

Objection. Assumes multiple discussions.

I don't remember.

Do you remember when you had such discussion or discussions?

No.

When did Publishing House make the decision to add a disclaimer to the second edition that some of the works, the authenticity of some of the works was questioned?

Sometime before it was printed.

What was your role in that decision?

Objection. Assumes that he had a role in that decision.

If any.

I don't remember exactly.

Who within Publishing House made the decision to include this disclaimer in Art, second edition?

I really don't know. It could've been me.

Who else within Publishing House did you consult on that issue?

Objection. Assumes he consulted.

If anyone.

I don't know. I don't remember.

Did Gallery Owner ever tell you that she thought it was inappropriate to include that disclaimer in Art, second edition?

I think she did.

Do you recall when she told you that?

No.

Do you recall what she said on that topic?

No.

Do you recall if anyone else was involved in that discussion?

I don't think so.

Do you recall what you said in response to her?

No.

Do you recall if she ever discussed with you the possibility of having parties other than her review the questioned works of art?

No.

Did you ever suggest that possibility?

No.

Did you ever come to learn that Gallery Owner was involved in the sale of any of the works in <u>Art</u> whose authenticity was questioned?

No.

No one ever told you that?

I heard that she was involved, allegedly involved in the sale of some paintings that were questioned. Whether they were in <u>Art</u> is another question.

From whom did you hear that she was allegedly involved in the sale of some works that were questioned?

I don't know.

I'm sorry?

I don't remember where I heard it.

Did there come a point in time that you learned Gallery Owner had been convicted in criminal court of a felony?

Yes.

When did you learn that?

I don't remember.

Was it before or after the publication of <u>Art</u>?

After.

Do you recall how you came to learn that?

I think a newspaper article was sent to me.

Do you remember who sent it?

I think Art Writer sent it.

Do you remember what your reaction was when you received those newspaper articles?

I tried to read them, but they were very fuzzy, and I just put them in a pile. Dismissed it.

Do you recall responding to Art Writer as to your interest in those newspaper articles?

No.

Sir, I'd ask you to review what has been marked as evidence. And the reason I'm asking you to review this exhibit is to see whether it refreshes your recollection that these are the newspaper articles that Art Writer had forwarded to you regarding Gallery Owner's felony conviction.

I'd just like to state an objection that there has been no indication that his memory needs to be refreshed.

This looks like the article that I already referred to.

And do you have difficulty reading these articles in front of you now, sir?

Yes.

Are you not able to read them?

They are pretty messy.

The question, sir, is are you able to read them.

I can start on them. Whether I can read the whole thing or not, I don't know.

Let's take the first page. Can you tell me at what point you're unable to read that article? What's the last sentence you can make out?

Objection. Counsel, are you intending to sit here and have him read these documents? If so, we can take a break and - -

Counsel, your witness testified that he was unable to read these articles when he received them.

That's incorrect.

That's not his testimony?

If you want to go back to his testimony, he started at it, and put it aside. He never said he was not able. Also, these are not the articles that were physically, actually received by Publisher through his fax machine or however they were communicated to him.

That's interesting, because they were produced from his files.

They are photocopies.

Well, if they are photocopies, if anything, they should be poorer quality.

I don't understand why - -

It's a question of the witness's credibility.

Let the record reflect that he's following a line of questions based on an answer that he is incorrectly reciting. Publisher has not stated that he is unable to read these. He stated that he put them aside. Is there some reason why you're asking him to go through this, apart from trying to impeach his credibility?

To refresh his recollection, also.

He hasn't stated that he doesn't remember. He stated he didn't read it. You can't refresh the recollection of someone who hasn't read the article.

You've testified enough. Now let's let the witness testify. Have you read the article?

I'm not sure. There are some lines here that are pretty badly messed up, and I can't say that for sure.

What percentage of the article can you read?

Objection. This is not an estimation exercise. He's not here to give you percentages.

Ninety percent?

Objection. Assumes that a percentage indicates coherency.

You can answer the question, sir.

Most of it is legible.

Thank you, sir. Now, since your counsel has indicated that I misunderstood your earlier answer, why - - strike that - - what did you do upon receipt of evidence?

I think I tried to read part of it, and then I put it aside, or gave it to somebody else.

Did you keep it in your files?

I didn't throw it away.

Were you in any way surprised by what you read in these articles?

Yes.

Do you remember whether or not you thanked Art Writer for sending you these articles?

I don't remember.

Did you appreciate that he had sent these articles to you?

Might have.

Don't remember?

No, not really.

Sir, I've had the court reporter put in front of you evidence. First I'd ask you if that's your handwriting?

Yes, it is.

Can you read that short note into the record, sir?

Objection. The document speaks for itself. Is there something that you can't read about it, Counsel?

Counsel, we could have been done by now.

It's clearly legible.

It's his handwriting. I want it read into the record.

It's perfectly legible. You're asking overreaching questions, and I need to put a limit to it.

No you don't, Counsel. If you want to call the judge, I'm very happy to
do that. Please answer the question, sir.

And the question is?

Could you read this note into the record that is your handwriting?

Say that again?

Could you read this note into the record that is your handwriting?

Yes I could.

Would you do that, please?

"Hi Art Writer. Egad, what a story. Yes, indeed I want this for my files.
Thanks very much and have a nice holiday. Sincerely, Publisher."

Are you able to recall, sir, whether or not you sent this fax to Art Writer
in response to receiving the documents that have been marked as
evidence?

It looks like my fax number is up here, so, probably I did.

In fact, it was sent on the same date that you received evidence, wasn't it?

I don't know when I received evidence.

Well, why don't we put evidence back in front of you so you can see the date on that. That might refresh your recollection.

It might.

Do you see the date on that fax, sir?

Yes, I do.

Does it appear that you sent what's been marked as evidence on the same day that you received evidence?

Foundation.

Yes.

Do you recall discussing with any of the employees of Publishing House the information that you learned when you received evidence?

No.

Is it your memory that you did not discuss - -

I don't remember.

Okay. Let me ask a different question. Do you recall ever discussing with any of the employees of Publishing House, Gallery Owner's felony conviction?

I don't remember specifically when or who I discussed it with.

Do you recall that you did discuss it with one or more of your employees?

Probably did.

When you say you probably did, why do you think you probably did?

Because I forwarded the information on to my legal counsel.

I'm not looking for any discussions you had with your legal counsel. I'm limiting my questions solely to employees of your company. Did you ever discuss with any of the employees of your company whether or not Gallery Owner's felony conviction should be taken into account, in light of the allegation that there were fakes pictured in Art?

No.

Never came up?

Don't think so.

Do you recall if in your own mind you believed Gallery Owner's felony conviction should be taken into account in assessing the issue of including in Art, second edition works whose authenticity, or alleged Artist works whose authenticity was questioned?

That was a legal question.

The relevance of Ms. Gallery Owner's felony conviction was a legal question?

Are we talking about the disclaimer?

No, sir. Let me rephrase my question. When you made the decision - - when you made the decision to publish <u>Art</u>, second edition, in making that decision, did you in any way take into account Gallery Owner's felony conviction?

No.

In making the decision about <u>Art</u>, second edition, did you take into account anything that Art Writer had told you?

I don't think so.

In making a decision about <u>Art</u>, second edition, did you take into account anything Art Critic had told you?

No.

Did anything that Art Writer told you affect the timing of your decision about <u>Art</u>, second edition?

No.

Did anything that Art Critic told you affect the timing of your decision about <u>Art</u>, second edition?

No.

Did anything that Art Writer told you affect any decision you made about any other works by Gallery Owner?

No.

Did anything that Art Critic told you affect the decision to publish or not publish any other works of Gallery Owner?

No.

Have you ever heard of the Artist Family Trust?

Yes.

What do you know about that organization?

Very little.

Tell me what you do know.

They seem to be associated with Art Writer and Art Critic.

Anything else?

That they include some members of the family.

Anything else?

That they are asserting some copyright ownerships.

What is your understanding of what copyright ownerships are being asserted by the Artist Family Trust?

That's as far as it goes. I don't know any more than that.

Are you aware of any impact on any decision you made regarding any books by Gallery Owner, whether to publish them or not publish them, that was affected in any way by the position the Artist Family Trust took on copyright issues?

No.

Are you aware of any communication or action of the Artist Family Trust that affected in any way Publishing House's decision to not publish any works that Gallery Owner approached your firm about publishing?

No.

Are you aware of any delay by Publishing House in publishing any work that it did publish by Gallery Owner that was caused in any way by any statements or actions of the Artist Family Trust?

No.

Have you ever heard of an organization called Art Organization?

Vaguely.

What if anything do you know about Art Organization?

Doesn't that refer to some galleries or something? Art association or something?

That's as much as you know about that organization?

Yes.

Do you know about any affiliation between the organization Art Organization and Art Critic?

Vaguely. I think that's one of her trade names or something. I don't know.

Are you aware of any actions or communications of Art Organization that affected in any way your decision about <u>Art?</u>

No.

Are you aware of any actions or communications of Art Organization that in any way impacted the timing of your decision about <u>Art?</u>

No.

Are you aware of any actions or communications of Art Marketing

Company that influenced in any way your decision about <u>Art</u>?

No.

Are you aware of any statements or actions by Art Marketing Company that affected the timing of your decision about <u>Art</u>?

No.

Have you ever heard of an organization called American Art, Incorporated?

Yes.

What is your knowledge of that organization?

I think that Art Critic has, is associated with that.

Are you aware of any communications or actions of American Art, Incorporated that affected in any way your decision about <u>Art</u>?

No.

Are you aware of any communications or actions of American Art, Incorporated that affected the timing of your decision about <u>Art</u>?

No.

Have you ever heard of Artist's Daughter?

I think I've seen the name.

Are you aware of any communications or actions by Artist's Daughter that in any way influenced your decision about <u>Art</u>?

No.

Are you aware of any actions by Artist's Daughter, including communications, that affected in any way the timing of your decision about <u>Art</u>?

No.

Have you ever received any communications, to your knowledge, from Artist's Daughter?

I don't think so.

Have you ever met this woman?

I don't remember ever meeting her.

Have you ever heard of any publishing house that goes by the name Publishing Company?

Yes.

Are you aware of any communications or actions of Publishing Company that have affected your decision about <u>Art</u>?

No.

Are you aware of any communications or actions by Publishing Company that affected the timing of your decision about <u>Art</u>?

No.

After you sent Art Writer the exhibit that's been marked as evidence, do you remember having any conversations with him about that note?

I don't remember them, no.

Do you remember if you had any conversation with Art Writer at all about the articles that he sent you, the newspaper articles that he sent you that are included in evidence?

I don't recall any.

Is it possible that you had some, but you just don't recall them?

That's right.

When do you recall Gallery Owner first discussing with you, if you recall at all, the possibility that she would file a lawsuit against Art Writer and Art Critic?

I don't remember when it was.

Do you recall that there was at least one such conversation?

Yes.

In fact, didn't you try to talk her out of it?

I did.

Do you recall what you said to her with regard to why you thought she shouldn't file such a lawsuit?

I advised against it.

Do you remember why you advised against it?

I said, "Even if you're right, it'll cost more than it's worth."

Do you recall anything else you told her?

No.

Do you recall anything she said in response to you?

That she was going to go ahead with it.

Did she explain to you why she was going to go ahead with it?

Yes.

What did she tell you?

"A matter of honor."

Do you recall her telling you anything else?

No.

Do you recall discussing with Art Writer the issue of litigation between him and Gallery Owner?

Very vaguely.

What do you recall?

Not much of anything.

Do you recall whether or not Art Writer encouraged you in your efforts to persuade Gallery Owner not to file litigation?

I don't remember.

It's possible, you just don't remember?

Yes.

Sir, I'm going to hand you what's been marked as evidence and ask you if you recall ever having seen that document before.

I think I saw it.

Do you recall discussing this letter with Managing Editor?

No, I don't.

Is Managing Editor still an employee of your company?

Yes.

Do you recall what impact if any this letter had on your company's business relationship with Gallery Owner?

We were not terribly concerned with Gallery Owner's scholarship. We were interested in the pictures. This was an art book.

And by "this," you're referring to evidence?

Yes.

Sir, the court reporter has handed you a document that has been marked as evidence. I'll ask you to review that to see if you recall having seen that before.

Yes, I have.

At the time that you received this document and thereafter, did the document or any of the issues that it raises have any impact on your company's business relationship with Gallery Owner?

This was merely an amusing letter.

What was amusing about it?

It speaks for itself.

You didn't take this letter seriously, is that correct, sir?

I didn't stop <u>Art</u> because of it.

In fact, you went forward with the publication of the second edition, isn't that right?

I did.

And did any of the contractual terms between Publishing House and Gallery Owner change because of anything in this evidence?

Vague, and no foundation.

I don't know what they would be.

Did you pay Gallery Owner or agree to pay her any lower royalty because of anything in this letter?

No.

Did you change any of the financial terms with Gallery Owner because of anything in this letter?

No.

Did you ever discuss the contents of this evidence with Art Writer?

I don't think so.

Did you ever discuss any of the contents with Art Critic?

I don't think so.

Did you ever discuss any of the contents of this evidence with Gallery Owner?

I don't remember if I did.

Do you recall discussing it with any of your employees?

I don't think so.

From the first sentence of this evidence, there is reference to a meeting about paintings. Do you recall that meeting at all?

Yes.

Do you recall where it took place?

My offices.

In California?

Yes.

Do you recall what was discussed at that meeting?

A little bit.

What do you recall?

Paintings, books, Gallery Owner.

Anything else?

I don't remember.

What do you recall being discussed about Gallery Owner?

I remember her being a topic of conversation, but I don't remember anything specific.

Do you recall if the topic came up regarding the inclusion of fakes in Art?

I don't remember.

Do you recall if Gallery Owner's felony conviction came up?

I don't remember.

You don't recall any of the details?

I really don't.

Sir, the reporter has handed you what's been marked as evidence. I'll ask you to review that to determine if you've ever seen that before.

Yes, I've seen it.

There is a reference in the first sentence of that document to a suggestion by you that Publishing House work with Art Writer on a new Artist book. Do you recall having any such discussion with Art Writer?

I think I discussed an Artist book with him, yes.

And do you recall that that was an idea initiated by you?

No, I don't.

Okay. In this memorandum it, the first sentence, and I'll just read it, says, "We were flattered at your suggestion that we work with you on a new Artist book, the," open quote, "brainstorm," close quote, "that you had in the shower." Does that refresh your recollection whether or not the suggestion came from you?

No.

Is it possible that the suggestion came from you, and you just don't remember?

Yes.

Do you recall who you had a conversation with about the possibility of Art Writer or Art Critic or Art Organization being involved in a new Artist book?

What was that question again?

I'll rephrase it. Do you remember whether it was Art Writer that you had the discussion with about the possibility of a new Artist book?

I don't remember.

It could have been, you just don't recall?

It could have been either one or both of them.

Art Writer or Art Critic?

Yes.

Do you recall what type of Artist book was discussed?

Something different than what we had. But - -

That's as much as you can recall?

Uh-huh.

I'm sorry?

That's all I recall.

In this evidence there is a reference to plagiarism in <u>Art</u>. Do you recall having any discussion with Art Writer or Art Critic regarding the alleged plagiarism?

Yes.

What do you recall about those discussions?

That they asserted that it happened.

Did you or anyone at your direction at Publishing House undertake any investigation as to whether or not there was any plagiarism in <u>Art</u>?

No, we didn't.

Why not?

Because the book was already out. The reviews had been very favorable from the art world, and we had sold out the whole edition.

In preparing <u>Art</u>, second edition, did you or anyone at your direction at

Publishing House undertake any investigation on this issue of plagiarism?

No.

Why not?

I'll state again, that the reviews had been very favorable and the edition sold out. Everyone in the art world that seemed to matter, that had seen the book, had liked it.

Did any of your employees ever raise with you a concern with regard to <u>Art</u>, second edition, that there might be copyright issues involved in publishing a second edition that contained plagiarism?

I don't think it was an issue.

Do you recall ever discussing that issue with any of your employees?

No.

Do you recall ever discussing the issue of plagiarism with Gallery Owner, at any time? Either in relation to <u>Art</u> or the second edition?

I don't remember.

Is it correct, then, as you sit here today, to your knowledge Publishing House made no investigation of whether or not there was any plagiarism included in <u>Art</u> while publishing the second edition?

We didn't do any fact-checking on the book.

Did anyone check the book published by Art Professor to see if any of the passages contained in <u>Art</u> were plagiarized from Art Professor's book?

Objection. Assumes facts not in evidence. No foundation. Vague as to which book and which edition of which book by Art Professor.

To my knowledge, no.

Why not?

This book was basically an art book with pictures. We only published the book because of the pictures. The text was lightweight. Didn't matter.

We have been going an hour and a half. Let's take a five-minute break.

Sure.

(Brief recess.)

Sir, the reporter has handed you a document marked as evidence. I'll ask you to review that to determine if that's your handwriting.

Yes.

Do you recall sending this note to Art Writer?

Looks like I did.

Do you recall if you did visit the gallery in New York after sending this note?

I didn't, no.

Any particular reason why not?

I didn't go to New York.

Sir, I'll ask you to review evidence to determine if you recall having seen that before.

For the record, Paragraph 2 refers to attached letters, which are not included.

Understood.

Off the record a sec.

(Discussion off the record.)

I don't remember receiving this.

We may be able to mark another exhibit that may or may not jog your memory. Sir, I'll hand you what's been marked as evidence. It appears to be, on the first page, the same as earlier evidence. But it also has attachments to it. I'd ask you to review that document with its attachments to determine whether or not that refreshes your memory about having received this document.

For the record, it should be noted that there is a large black band that occludes careful and thorough reading of the words on all of these documents.

I think I've seen this before.

Do you recall what if any reaction you had to this document when you received it?

I don't remember any reaction to it.

Did you take any steps or instruct any of your employees to take any steps in response to receiving this document?

I don't think so.

Do you recall discussing any of the contents of evidence with Art Writer?

I don't remember.

Do you recall discussing any of the contents with Gallery Owner?

No.

Is it fair to say that this document was unimportant to you?

That's fair to say.

Sir, the reporter has handed you a multi-page document that has been marked as evidence. My first question to you is do you recall ever having seen either the cover letter or any of the other pages contained within evidence?

I probably saw this stuff, yes.

Do you have any understanding as to why these materials were sent to Gallery Owner?

It looks like these are legal bills, which would back up legal expenses.

Do you have any understanding as to why legal expenses of Publishing House would be forwarded to Gallery Owner?

Her contract indemnifies, indemnifies the publisher.

And that indemnification includes for attorney's fees?

Yes.

I'll ask you to review the document that's been marked as evidence, and my first question will be whether you recall having seen that document before.

I don't remember seeing it.

Do you recall learning from either General Manager or any of your other employees that Gallery Owner had informed your company that her insurance carrier would not be reimbursing Publishing House for its legal expenses?

No.

Do you recall discussing that issue at all with anyone?

No.

Do you know in fact whether or not Gallery Owner has reimbursed your company for any legal fees it has incurred?

I think not. But I don't know for sure.

Who within your company would know?

General Manager.

Sir, I've asked the reporter to mark and hand you evidence. I'll ask you to review that two-page exhibit to determine whether you recall having seen any portion of it before.

I believe that was shown to me, yes.

Do you recall discussing this letter with General Manager, either before or after it was sent?

No.

Do you recall giving your approval to the sending of this letter?

No.

Do you recall anyone asking for your approval?

No.

Do you recall any of your employees at Publishing House discussing with you what the language was to be used as a disclaimer in <u>Art</u>, second edition?

Well, that was a legal matter.

I'm not asking for communications with your attorneys, but do you recall any communications with your employees on that topic?

As to what the disclaimer should say?

Yes, sir.

No.

I've asked the reporter to hand you a document that's been marked as evidence. I'll ask you to review that to determine if you recall ever having seen it before.

I might have seen that. I'm not sure.

All right, sir. Directing your attention to the discussion in this letter about Gallery Owner's claim that she had not received royalties for two years, are you familiar with whether or not that is an accurate statement, as of the date of this letter?

No, I don't know.

Who within your company would know?

This was addressed to General Manager. I would assume that he would know.

Let me just counsel my client not to make assumptions. They really only want to know what you know.

That's absolutely true. In the third paragraph of this letter, there is a reference to the possible closing of Gallery Owner's gallery. Do you recall ever discussing, first of all, with Gallery Owner the possibility that she would be closing her gallery?

I have a recollection that I heard that she might be closing the gallery.

Let's take it one step at a time. Do you remember discussing that with her?

No.

Do you recall ever discussing that with General Manager?

No.

Do you recall any other identifiable person that you recall - -

No.

- - the possibility that Gallery Owner's gallery might be closed? I'm sorry?

No.

Do you know whether the gallery is closed?

I think it's still open.

What's your basis for thinking that?

I called the gallery.

How recently?

A week ago.

Do you recall who answered the phone when you called?

Gallery Owner.

What was the topic of discussion last time you called her?

I told her that the third edition had, that I had a copy for her.

Did you discuss anything else in this telephone call?

I don't remember anything else.

Prior to today have you had any discussions with Gallery Owner about the deposition that you were to give in this case?

No.

Have you had any discussions with anyone who identified themselves as an attorney for Gallery Owner about your deposition in this case?

No.

How about a paralegal?

No.

Had you ever met Gallery Owner's Lawyer before today?

No.

Do you recall Gallery Owner ever discussing with you any problem she was having with a publisher, other than Publishing House, in obtaining her royalty payments that she thought were due?

In this letter she mentions Publishing Corporation, here.

Do you recall ever discussing any royalty problems she was having with Publishing Corporation with Gallery Owner?

Maybe a mention.

Do you recall anything about that discussion?

No.

Do you recall if she ever said anything to you about transparencies that Publishing Corporation had that it shouldn't have used in some way?

Yes.

What do you recall about that?

Simply that she had, she got back copies of transparencies instead of originals, from them.

Do you recall when she told you that?

No.

Do you recall if she told you whether she ever confronted Publishing Corporation about that?

I don't remember.

Sir, the reporter has marked the next document as evidence. I'll ask you to look at that to determine if you recall ever having seen it before.

I don't know whether I've seen it before.

Do you recognize this as a form of report that is prepared within your company?

Yes.

Who would be knowledgeable within your company about this type of report?

General Manager.

Sir, I'm going to hand you what's been marked as evidence and ask you to review that document to determine if you recall ever having seen it before.

For the record, the title of the letterhead is missing.

I think we can all stipulate it's Art Lawyer.

I think we can do that.

Yes.

Do you recall discussing this letter with any of your employees?

No.

Do you recall what actions if any you took in response to this letter?

No.

Do you recall what impact if any this letter had on Publishing House's interest and involvement in <u>Art</u>, second edition?

No noticeable impact.

Do you recall any impact of any type?

No.

The court reporter has handed you another letter that has been marked as evidence, which again, I think counsel will agree, is an Art Lawyer letterhead letter. Do you recall having seen this letter before, sir?

Yes.

Do you recall what response if any you made to this letter?

No response to it.

Do you recall what impact if any this letter had on any of the efforts of your company with regard to <u>Art</u>?

None.

The court reporter has handed to you a multi-page document marked as evidence. It says on the first page, "Agreement." Do you recall signing this agreement, sir?

Yes.

On the first page of this exhibit there are some handwritten notes in the upper right-hand corner. Do you recognize any of that handwriting?

It looks like mine.

Could you just read the part that looks like your handwriting?

"Gallery Owner, please, re, signed by back, ASAP."

Do you have any understanding what that note means?

Seems like something might be missing. Shall I speculate?

Please do not speculate. He only wants to know what you know.

Do you know? Do you have any understanding of what that note means? And if you don't, that's fine. I understand.

For the record, the witness is giving it a long, good think.

If you want me to speculate, I'll speculate.

We don't want you to speculate.

We don't want you to speculate. If you - -

Then I have nothing to say.

Do you recognize the handwriting just below what you read into the record?

No.

Sir, the reporter has handed you evidence. I'll ask you to review that letter to determine whether you recall ever having seen that before.

I don't remember seeing this.

Do you recall any discussions at any time with either Art Writer or Art Critic in which you expressed shock or surprise at plagiarism being present in <u>Art</u>?

Objection. It assumes plagiarism is in evidence. It's not. Lacks foundation.

You may answer the question.

I only looked at the pictures. I didn't deal with the text.

Is it correct, then, that as you sit here today you don't recall discussing in any way the issue of plagiarism as it might relate to <u>Art</u>?

Indeed I may have discussed that issue sometime, with someone. I don't remember.

And you may have discussed that issue with Art Writer?

May have.

Do you recall ever discussing with anyone whether <u>Art</u> was used to authenticate a fake that was purchased for a significant sum of money?

I don't think I ever discussed that with anyone.

Sir, the reporter has handed you a two-page document that has been marked as evidence. I'll ask you first to review that to determine if you recall ever having seen it before.

I think I saw that, yes.

Do you recall discussing any of the contents of this document with Gallery Owner?

I think I turned this over to my attorney.

Do you recall discussing this litigation at any time with Gallery Owner?

No.

Have you ever met Gallery Owner's Husband?

Yes.

Do you recall ever discussing with Gallery Owner's Husband anything about Art Writer?

I may have.

Do you recall any statements that Gallery Owner's Husband ever made to you about Art Writer?

No.

Do you recall any statements he ever made to you about Art Critic?

No.

Do you recall any statements he ever made to you about the Artist Family Trust?

No.

Do you recall Gallery Owner's Husband ever telling you that he believed Art Writer was interfering in the affairs of his wife's gallery?

No.

Sir, the reporter has marked the next exhibit as evidence. I'll ask you to review that to determine if you recall ever having seen that before.

I don't remember seeing this.

Do you remember discussing with General Manager or any other Publishing House employee any royalty dispute with Gallery Owner?

Yes.

What do you recall about that discussion?

I put it in the hands of General Manager to handle in a proper manner.

Did he ever report back to you on how he had handled that?

Yes.

What did he report back to you?

That he handled it in a proper manner.

Did he give you any of the details of how he handled it?

I think he showed me correspondence.

Do you recall anything else?

No.

The reporter has marked the next exhibit as evidence. Do you recall having seen that before?

When you say "that," Counsel, do you mean the entire document, or some portion of it?

Any portion of it.

I think that I have seen this, yes.

Do you recall having any discussions with Art Writer or Art Critic about possible use by your company of the Artist Family Trust seal?

No.

Do you recall having any discussions with anyone else about the possible use by your company of the Artist Family Trust seal?

No.

Did you ever consider that possibility?

No.

Why not?

I never met anybody from the Artist Family Trust. I didn't know anything about them. It never, it wasn't an issue for me.

It just wasn't something you were interested in?

Right.

Did you ever tell Art Writer or Art Critic that you were interested in - -

No.

- - doing business with the Artist Family Trust?

Never said that.

Did you ever tell them you were interested?

I was interested in the paintings. Period.

You didn't care about the Trust?

I didn't know anything about the Trust.

Is that still true until today?

Until today.

The reporter has marked the next document as evidence. Do you recall seeing this document before, or any portion of it?

Yes.

Do you recall discussing it or any portion of it with anyone?

Yes.

Who do you recall discussing it with?

Gallery Owner sent this to me.

And what do you recall discussing about this document with Gallery Owner?

Simply that this was a letter that she was glad that she had kept.

Do you recall discussing any copyright issues with Gallery Owner, in relation to this letter?

Yes.

What do you recall about that?

<u>Art</u>, third edition.

And what do you recall about discussing <u>Art</u>, third edition with Gallery Owner?

There was a question about the text in <u>Art</u>, third edition, and Gallery Owner thought that this letter covered both the text and the pictures.

When you say - -

In terms of copyright.

When you say there was a question about the text in <u>Art</u>, third edition, do you mean by that to refer to a book published by your company. Or are you referring - -

Potentially to be published by my company.

And in fact, has your company published such a book?

We published the pictures.

But no text?

Right.

Do you recall anything else about this exhibit that you discussed with Gallery Owner?

No, I don't think so.

I'll hand you what's been marked as evidence. I'll ask you to review that document to determine if you recall ever having seen it before.

Yes, I saw that letter.

In the first sentence there is reference to a recent call by you to Gallery Owner's Husband. Do you have any memory as to what that sentence is referring to?

No.

Do you recall having any telephone conversation with Gallery Owner's Husband?

No.

Do you recall communicating any support to Gallery Owner regarding any issue, in the fall of last year?

Say that again?

Do you recall communicating any support to Gallery Owner in the fall of last year?

No.

Do you recall offering any support to Gallery Owner's Husband - -

No.

- - in the fall of last year?

No.

There is a book, or potential book, mentioned in this letter, <u>Art</u>, fourth edition. Do you recall whether or not your company considered the possible publication of that book?

We did.

Do you recall if any discussion has been made on the possible publication of that book?

We decided not to do it.

What were the reasons for the decision not to do it?

I don't remember.

Were any communications by any third parties or any actions by any third parties any part of the reasons why your company decided not to publish that book?

No.

Sir, the reporter has handed you the next document that has been marked as evidence. I'll ask you to review that document to determine if you recall having seen it before.

I think I've seen it before.

Is that your signature at the bottom of that letter?

Uh-huh.

I'm sorry?

Yes.

As to that exhibit, sir, your letter makes reference to "friendly and good-natured talks, before the lawsuit, both on the phone and in person." What do you recall about such talks?

Friendly and good-natured.

And you're referring to talks with Art Writer and Art Critic?

Yes.

And in those talks were there ever discussions of Gallery Owner?

Yes.

Do you recall what discussions of Gallery Owner there were in those talks?

Yes.

What do you recall?

I remember a discussion of some errors that were allegedly in <u>Art</u>.

What else do you recall?

The discussions of their gallery.

Focusing specifically on comments about Gallery Owner, do you recall any other comments about Gallery Owner?

I think they, I think they mentioned the clippings that we saw previously, about her lawsuit.

Her lawsuit, or her felony conviction?

Her felony conviction.

Anything else?

They talked about doing an Artist book themselves. And I think they did one.

Referring to Gallery Owner's felony conviction, do you recall if anyone ever told you what the crime was that she was convicted of?

I have a very vague memory of the matter.

What's your memory?

And - -

Wait. Are you answering the question?

Am I answering the question? I have a vague memory of a discussion about it.

And what is your memory of what crimes she was convicted of?

Actually, I don't remember that.

Do you recall anyone ever telling you that it was theft by deception?

No.

Is it correct that early this year you were still willing to discuss with Art Writer and Art Critic the possibility of Publishing House publishing an Artist book by them?

Yes. I did discuss with them an Artist book.

To be published by your company, potentially?

Yes.

Do you recall what their response was?

I don't remember. We discussed future works by Artist and how they might come out.

Off the record for a second.

(Discussion off the record.)

Sir, I'm handing you documents that have been marked as evidence. Do you recall ever being requested by Gallery Owner to throw away or destroy any document that she had sent to you?

No.

Do you recall ever doing that?

No.

Referring your attention to this evidence, and to the second page, do you recall ever having seen a different version of that particular document?

Objection. No foundation that he's seen this document.

All right, let's ask that. Do you recall ever having seen this document before?

I have a vague recollection of having seen this one. Very vague.

Do you have any recollection of having received, on the same day, two different versions of this document?

No.

Do you have a recollection of having received a prior version of this document that was completely typewritten, such that the handwriting that appears about two-thirds of the way down in the second paragraph wasn't there, but was instead typewritten words?

No.

Do you recall receiving a prior version of this document where Gallery Owner accused Art Writer and Art Critic of criminal conduct?

No.

No foundation.

Do you recall having any telephone discussions with Gallery Owner in which she asked you to destroy a document that she had sent you?

No.

Do you recall ever discussing with any of your employees any request from Gallery Owner that you destroy a document that she had sent you?

No.

And as you sit here today, you don't recall one way or the other whether you did in fact destroy a document at the request of Gallery Owner?

I'd say I didn't.

I'll represent to you that the prior version of this document is not in your files.

Counsel, that is argumentative. Where it may be is another question. You've asked him whether he destroyed anything, and the answer can be no.

Well, we can put your document production in front of him, and he can try to go through it and see if he can find a prior version of this letter.

Counsel, there are other options besides him destroying something. There could be filing problems. There could be all kinds of things. This is harassing.

No, it's a question.

He's answered it. Move on.

I will move on when I'm ready, Counsel.

My client is not here to be harassed.

He's here to testify.

Yes.

And I'm examining him.

And he's answered your last question. Move on.

I've got more questions. I'm not done.

Please proceed, then.

Do you recall having a telephone conversation with Gallery Owner in which you told her that you had destroyed the document that she sent you?

No.

Don't recall that at all?

No.

You're saying that it never happened?

I don't recall it happening. I don't think I did.

Is it possible that it happened?

Well, anything, almost, is possible, but I don't have any recollection of this.

So as you sit here today you don't remember ever destroying any document at Gallery Owner's request?

Asked and answered.

Asked and answered.

First, sir, I'll ask you if you recall ever having seen the document that's been marked as evidence before?

I don't remember seeing it.

Who is Associate Editor?

He is an editor.

Of your company?

Yes.

And who is Royalties Clerk?

She is the person in charge of royalties. Payments and statements.

Again, at your company?

Yes.

The reporter has handed you a document marked as evidence. I'll ask you to review that to determine whether you remember ever having seen it before.

Yes, I think I saw it.

Do you recall ever discussing with Gallery Owner any, quote, "mildly intimidating," close quote, letters that you had received from Art Writer?

Would you repeat that, please?

Sure. Do you recall ever discussing with Gallery Owner any, quote, "mildly intimidating," close quote, letters that you had received from Art Writer?

I believe I discussed Art Writer's letters with Gallery Owner.

Do you recall what you said to her about those letters?

Yes. That they were trying to get me to not publish <u>Art</u>, second edition.

And do you recall what you said to her with regard to the effect those letters were having on that decision about <u>Art</u>, second edition?

That it would not affect my decision.

Do you recall anything she said in response to that?

No, I don't remember.

Did there ever come a time that you told Gallery Owner that any of the letters or correspondence from Art Writer or Art Lawyer were having an effect on your decision of what works of Gallery Owner's to publish?

I don't think I ever told her that, that we were dissuaded from publishing, due to some letters.

And in fact, were you ever dissuaded from publishing - -

No.

- - due to any of those letters?

No.

Did Gallery Owner ever tell you whether any other publishers had taken her books off the market?

Yes.

What did she tell you in that regard?

That Publishing Corporation had discontinued her photography book.

Other than telling you that Publishing Corporation had discontinued her photography book, did she ever tell you of any other decisions by any other publisher to keep her books off the market?

I think the Artist's Daughter book was also published by them, and they stopped publishing it.

By Publishing Corporation?

Yes.

Any others?

Not that I know.

Do you know why she believed Publishing Corporation had stopped publishing her photography book?

I really don't remember.

Did she ever tell you what she believed were the reasons why Publishing Corporation stopped publishing the Artist's Daughter book?

I don't remember.

In this letter marked as evidence there is a request that you provide copies of letters to Gallery Owner's attorneys. Did you in fact provide copies of those letters to her attorneys?

I don't remember whether we did or not.

Do you recall whether - - strike that. Do you recall ever discussing with Gallery Owner whether, in your opinion, those letters provide any basis for a lawsuit by Gallery Owner? And by those letters, I'm referring to letters from Art Writer and Art Lawyer.

No.

Did you ever discuss that topic with anyone within your company?

Don't think so.

I'll hand you what's been marked as evidence, sir, and ask you if you recall ever having seen that before.

I don't remember, I don't remember this.

Do you recognize any of the handwriting on it?

Looks like Gallery Owner's.

Do you recall whether or not you did take a trip abroad in the summer of last year?

I remember that distinctly, yes.

Do you recall if prior to that trip you forwarded or caused to be forwarded any letters from Art Writer or Art Lawyer to Gallery Owner's attorneys?

I don't remember.

The reporter has handed you a multi-page exhibit marked as evidence. I'll ask you to review it to determine if you recall ever having seen any of the contents of that before.

Counsel, aren't these redundant on what we have already seen?

They may be. But they were part of a duplicate production by your client.

Okay.

I think I've seen them.

You think you have?

Yes.

Did anything in these letters affect in any way your company's business relationship with Gallery Owner?

No.

For the record, they represent previous exhibits in evidence.

Thank you, Counsel. Sir, the reporter has handed you an exhibit marked as evidence. Do you recall ever having seen that before?

Yes.

In the third paragraph there is a reference to, quote, "Art Writer's allegations that he has virtually shut down my publishing efforts," close quote. Do you recall Art Writer ever saying to you that he had taken any steps with regard to Gallery Owner's publishing efforts?

I don't remember any allegations that Art Writer had virtually shut down her publishing efforts.

You don't recall anyone ever saying that to you?

Right.

Did your company ever consider the possibility of publishing
Contemporary Art, by Gallery Owner?

Yes.

What decision if any was made on that possibility?

We decided not to do it.

Do you recall why you decided not to do it?

It lacked sufficient merit.

Do you recall what criteria you relied on in reaching that decision?

No. I mean, we decided not to do it. It didn't have sufficient merit.

Was anyone else at your company involved in the decision not to do it?

No.

Why don't we go ahead and take a lunch break at this point. And you
want to reconvene in an hour, Counsel?

An hour. If we could begin promptly, I'd be very grateful.

(Luncheon recess taken for one hour.)

Sir, I'm going to hand you what's been marked as evidence. I'll ask you to review that to determine if you've ever seen it before.

I don't remember seeing that.

Do you remember at some point in early summer of last year learning that Gallery Owner was filing a lawsuit?

Yes.

Do you recall ever discussing with her any allegations that she intended to make or had made in that lawsuit regarding a monopoly?

No.

Do you recall ever discussing with her any type of antitrust claims?

No.

Sir, did your company ever obtain any type of license relating to Artist, from anyone?

A license?

Yes, sir.

No.

Do you recall anyone ever approaching Publishing House on the topic of granting your firm a license regarding Artist?

No.

You don't remember that ever happening?

No.

Do you remember Art Writer ever telling you that your company needed a license from anyone in order to publish art books related to Artist?

Absolutely not.

Do you remember anyone ever telling you - -

No. No.

Let me ask the question, sir. I appreciate your answer, but I do have to ask the complete question. Did anyone ever tell you or suggest to you that your company needed a license in order to publish anything having to do with Artist?

Never heard of such a thing.

Do you recall ever having any discussions with Gallery Owner about what industry practice was for credit lines for pictures, the type as in <u>Art</u>?

No.

Do you recall her ever stating in your presence, or to you, that she was aware of anyone having engaged in an unlawful practice with regard to the credits they listed for photographs in any art book?

Vague recollection.

What's your recollection, sir?

Vague.

Anything more about - -

No.

Who at Publishing House was responsible for determining what the credits would be for photographs in <u>Art</u>?

Nobody. We relied on the author.

So it's correct to say, then, that the credits that the author submitted are what you printed?

Yes.

For all the images in <u>Art</u>?

Yes.

Is that true for <u>Art</u> and <u>Art</u>, second edition?

Yes.

Sir, I'm going to hand you what's been marked as evidence and ask you to review that document to determine if you recall ever having seen it before.

I don't remember seeing this.

Do you recall ever discussing with Gallery Owner any claims that she believed she had for Art Critic or Art Writer using photographs that had been lifted from her books, from Gallery Owner's books?

I don't remember any discussions with her about that.

Do you remember any discussions with anyone about that?

No.

Do you recall yourself ever reviewing any book authored by Art Critic or Art Writer with an eye towards determining whether any of the pictures in that book were copied from <u>Art</u>?

No.

I'll hand you what's been marked as evidence, sir. Do you recall having seen this document before?

No, I don't.

Do you recall ever discussing with Gallery Owner the possibility of publishing a foreign language version of <u>Art</u>?

Yes.

Is that project still ongoing?

It was never terminated.

Do you know what plans if any Publishing House has today with regard to a foreign language publication of that book?

Let me interject, if it's a trade secret, you should not interject that. There is no reason for them to know what the plans for Publishing House are, without protection for confidentiality.

We do have a protective order for the case. So we can deal with that.

Well, we have no plans.

Thank you, sir. Was there a decision not to do that, or is that something that has just fallen by the wayside?

We're waiting for the foreign distributors.

Do you know what the foreign distributors are waiting on?

I haven't a clue.

I'll hand you what's been marked as evidence, sir. I'll ask if you recall ever seeing that document before?

I don't remember seeing this.

Do you recall ever discussing with Gallery Owner her belief that third parties were making false or misleading statements about her?

Yes.

What do you recall about those discussions?

That she said people were making false and misleading statements about her.

Let's take them one at a time. Did she tell you what any of those false statements were?

Yes, but I don't remember what they were.

Did she tell you who she thought was making them?

Yes.

Who did she tell you?

Art Critic and Art Writer.

Did she tell you why she thought that?

No.

Did you have any understanding as to why she thought that?

No.

Would your answers to those prior questions be any different if I changed "false" to "misleading"? And if you need me to ask the question again, I will.

My answers would be the same.

I'll hand you what's been marked as evidence. I'll ask you if you recall ever having seen this document before.

I haven't seen this before, I don't think.

All right, sir. Do you recall ever discussing with Gallery Owner the question of whether there were any works by Artist that as of summer two years ago were still under copyright?

No.

Do you recall ever discussing with Gallery Owner any works of Artist that as of summer two years ago were not in the public domain?

No.

Do you have any knowledge as to whether or not there were any works of Artist that were not in the public domain as of summer two years ago?

No.

Do you have any knowledge as to whether there were any works of Artist still under copyright in the summer of two years ago?

I'm not aware of any.

I'll hand you what's been marked as evidence. I'll ask you to review that to determine if you recall ever having seen it before.

I think I saw this.

Do you recall ever discussing with Gallery Owner the possibility of publishing her autobiography, <u>Vision of Artist</u>?

Yes.

And what was that decision?

That we couldn't do it.

Do you recall why you made that decision?

Yes.

Why.

It wouldn't sell.

Did you have any reason for believing it wouldn't sell?

Yes.

What was the reason?

Just for clarification, you mean beyond his experience, generally, as a publisher?

He can answer the question, Counsel.

If you can, answer the question. Objection on the grounds of vague and ambiguous.

My determination was that it wouldn't sell.

Was part of your determination based on the references to a ghost of Artist having been spotted in a grove of trees?

No.

Do you recall ever stating to anyone that you thought Gallery Owner was crazy for thinking she had seen Artist's ghost?

I don't remember. I don't remember that, no.

Is it possible that you said that?

It is possible.

But as you sit here today you don't remember one way or the other?

Right.

Did you ever discuss with Gallery Owner her belief that she had seen Artist's ghost?

Yes.

What do you recall about that discussion?

I didn't take it too seriously.

Did you tell her that?

Yes.

What was her reaction?

She was very gracious.

I'll hand you what's been marked as evidence. I'll ask you to review that to determine if you recall ever having seen it before.

I think I saw this.

Do you recall discussing it with Gallery Owner?

No.

Do you recall discussing it with anyone?

I think I just said "Put it in the author file."

Did anything contained in that letter have any impact on your business relationship with Gallery Owner?

No.

I'll hand you what's been marked as evidence, and I'll just ask you to review it long enough to answer the question whether you recall it or remember having seen it before.

No, I haven't seen this.

Thank you, sir. I'll hand you another exhibit. I'll ask if you recall ever having seen that document before.

No, I don't think I ever saw that.

I'll hand you what's been marked as evidence. I'll ask you if you recall ever having seen that document before.

For the record, it's an incomplete document, beginning on page 2, bearing the Copyright Lawyers letterhead.

And for the record, it's as produced by the witness's company.

I haven't seen this before.

All right, sir. Do you recall if any of the images in <u>Art</u> were copyrighted by a firm known as Art Owners, Incorporated?

I don't know.

Do you know if any of the images contained in <u>Art</u>, second edition are copyrighted by the firm Art Owners, Incorporated?

I don't know.

Do you know if your company has any license from Art Owners, Incorporated to reproduce any of its images in any edition of <u>Art</u>?

Objection. Assumes that there is some ownership interest of Art Owners, Incorporated.

Well, I don't have extra copies of it, but since you asked.

I didn't ask. I objected.

I take it as an implicit ask. Sir, who was responsible for preparing the credit section of <u>Art</u>, second edition?

Credit section? Let me see it.

I can't give it to you now, but I'll ask you to look at the very bottom of it.

For the record, he's handed the deponent - -

Wait. Do you want to mark it? We'll just mark it.

No, I want to put on the record what - -

Counsel, may I have it back? I only handed it to the witness as a courtesy. May I have it back?

Not until we figure out what it is.

If you want to read from that single page, feel free to say what it is.

No. I'll indicate what it is my client has just been handed.

I'm requesting that document back.

I'll be happy to give it to you after I've described what it is for the record.

I didn't introduce that document. It has my personal notes on it, attorney/client notes. I want it back.

No. You'll get it back after I've - -

I handed the last page of that document to the witness.

Maybe you don't understand. When you hand something to my client, I'm going to look at it.

And you're not going to look at every part.

Sit down, Counsel. Harassing me is not helpful.

Off the record.

No, I don't want to go off the record.

I do.

You handed my client a document, and I'm entitled - -

Fine. Do you want to play games? Play games, Counsel. Go ahead.

You handed my client a document. I'm entitled to look at it.

You're free to look at it.

You handed him a document that seems to be faxed from American Art, Incorporated in New York.

That is correct. That is correct.

It has as the heading, "<u>Art</u>."

As I said, Counsel - -

It is clipped to other documents.

As I said, we don't have a problem. You can use that entire document. Go ahead.

I will. And it has selected pages of <u>Art</u>, second edition. It is seven pages long.

I removed the page I was concerned about.

In the future, Counsel, I'm here to represent my client. And when you hand him documents, I'm going to look at them.

You do that, Counsel.

Now, is there a question pending?

Just remember, what goes around comes around. May I see that, please, sir?

Yes, you may hand him the document.

Let's mark this as an exhibit. Which is the document counsel just examined. I'll hand you this evidence, and ask you if you recognize any portion of that exhibit.

Yes.

What is that document?

It looks like the title page on the Publishing House book.

<u>Art</u>, second edition?

Yes.

Directing your attention to the last page of that exhibit - -

Yes.

- - is there, is there a footnote that discusses Art Owners, Incorporated?

Well, here is the name Art Owners, Incorporated, here.

Yes sir. And are you looking at the bottom note on that page, sir?

Next to the last one. Oh. The next to the last, and the last, yeah. And the third from the last.

And does that note refresh your recollection as to whether or not Art Owners, Incorporated owns the copyright to any of the images contained in this book?

No, it doesn't.

To your knowledge, would that information appear in your book if it was inaccurate?

Calls for speculation.

I didn't read this page in the book - -

Who did?

- - prior to today.

Who within your firm has responsibility to do that?

No one.

No one?

No.

Thank you. Who within your firm has responsibility to determine whether all necessary license rights are obtained before a book is published that requires any license rights?

Objection. There is an assumption that there was a requirement of some license rights at all.

You can answer the question.

You can.

When it's a question, we usually hand it to an outside party, because it's a technical matter. A copyright is complicated.

What outside party did you hand any licensing questions regarding <u>Art</u> to?

I don't think we did.

If your company had a license agreement with Art Owners, Incorporated, would it be your corporate practice to keep a copy of that license agreement in the company files?

Yes.

And who within your company would be responsible for making certain that that licensing agreement was in your company files?

Well, everybody is responsible for the integrity of the files.

Who is everybody? All 70 employees?

Uh-huh.

I'm sorry?

Yes.

So as you sit here right now you don't know whether or not your company has a license agreement from Art Owners, Incorporated for <u>Art</u>, second edition, or some portion of it, do you?

No.

Do you recall ever discussing the issue of the necessity of a license from Art Owners, Incorporated with Gallery Owner?

No.

Do you recall ever discussing that with any of your employees?

No.

Sir, I'm going to hand you what's been marked as evidence and ask you if you recall ever seeing that document before.

Yes.

Do you recall ever discussing this document with Gallery Owner?

No.

Do you recall ever discussing with Gallery Owner the issue of her ownership of any transparencies used in any books published by your firm?

Yes.

What do you recall about those discussions?

What a wonderful collection she had.

Anything else?

No.

Do you recall ever asking her for any evidence or confirmation of her ownership of those transparencies?

No.

Do you recall ever discussing with her whether or not any of the reproductions in <u>Art</u> came from transparencies owned by Art Critic?

No.

Do you recall ever discussing that with anyone?

No.

I'll hand you what's been marked as evidence, and ask you if you recall ever seeing that before.

I think I probably saw that.

Do you recall discussing that with Gallery Owner?

No, I don't.

Do you recall her ever telling you that she was having difficulty getting the necessary transparencies - -

Yes.

What do you recall discussing on that?

That she was having difficulty getting them.

Did she ever tell you what those difficulties were?

No.

Do you recall ever seeing this document that's been marked as evidence before, sir?

No.

What work did your firm undertake with regard to the possible publication of <u>Art Theory</u>?

First or second edition?

Let's take them one at a time. What edition if at all was your firm involved with on this particular book?

The second edition.

And did your firm publish that edition?

No.

And why didn't it publish it?

I didn't want to.

Why didn't you want to?

I didn't like it, particularly.

Was there any other reason? Do you recall any other reason you didn't publish that book?

No.

Do you recall ever seeing this evidence before, sir?

I think I saw it.

Do you recall ever discussing this letter with Gallery Owner?

Yes.

Did your firm publish the book that's listed as an item in this letter, called <u>Art for Kids</u>?

No, we did not.

Do you recall why your firm did not publish that book?

A mistake that I made.

What was that mistake?

I didn't look at it.

Any particular reason why you didn't look at it?

It was a children's book, and I don't read children's books. I send them to other people to look at.

Why do you characterize your failure to look at it as a mistake?

I think if I would have looked at it, I would have published it.

Did your firm or you discuss with Gallery Owner the possibility of publishing the book, <u>Artist: Collected Works</u>, an item on this exhibit?

I don't remember that one.

Sir, the reporter has handed you evidence. Do you recall ever seeing that document before?

I don't remember seeing this, no.

Okay.

Is Designer an employee of your company?

No.

Was he in early winter, two years ago?

No.

Is this the consultant that you referred to earlier in your testimony?

Yes.

Would you look at evidence to determine if you recall ever having seen that before?

I don't remember seeing it.

I'll hand you evidence and ask you if you recall ever having seen that before.

I don't remember seeing this.

I'll ask you to review evidence to determine if you recall having discussed with Gallery Owner in fall, two years ago, any possible infringement of <u>Art</u> by either Art Writer or Art Critic.

I don't remember talking about it with her.

Do you remember discussing it with anyone?

No.

Sir, will you review evidence to determine if you recall ever having seen it before?

I don't remember seeing it.

Do you recall discussing at any time between the summer of two years ago and the present whether or not you would support Gallery Owner in any litigation she filed against Art Writer or Art Critic?

Would you ask the question again?

Sure. Do you recall at any time, from the summer of two years ago through the present, discussing with Gallery Owner whether or not you would support her in litigation against Art Writer or Art Critic?

What do you mean by "support"?

Do you recall discussing with Gallery Owner any assistance you might provide her in any litigation against Art Writer or Art Critic?

No.

What do you recall discussing with Gallery Owner regarding possible litigation by her against Art Writer or Art Critic?

Told her not to get involved in a lawsuit on this issue.

Which issue is that, sir?

A dispute with Art Writer and Art Critic.

And do you recall anything else you told her?

I probably wished her the best of luck.

Anything else?

No.

Sir, I'll represent to you that this evidence includes a first page that you may have seen before today, but also includes some additional pages attached to it. I'll ask you to review that entire document to determine if you recall having seen it before.

I don't know what it is.

So you don't recall having seen it before?

No.

All right, sir. Thank you. Sir, the reporter has handed you a document marked as evidence. I'll ask you to review it to determine if you recall ever having seen it before.

Yes, I think I saw this letter.

Do you recall discussing any portion of this letter with Gallery Owner?

I might have.

What do you recall about that discussion?

I think I agreed that a lot of these errors were, as she quotes, "picayunish." Or as she says up here, "picayunish." Whatever that means.

And by "these errors," you mean that are set out in this exhibit?

Yes.

Do you recall anything else?

No.

Do you recall ever discussing with Gallery Owner, Art Writer's role as ex-officio watchdog for the Artist estate?

Did I ever hear him say that or her say that? No, I'm just reading it here.

Other than relying on this exhibit?

No.

In the last paragraph of the second page there is a reference to Art Writer, Art Critic, and company attempting to scare you into not publishing Art, second edition. Did you ever discuss that topic with Gallery Owner?

Yes.

And what do you recall about that discussion?

That my decision about Art would be my decision.

Anything else?

No.

Did you give assurances to Gallery Owner that nothing Art Writer, Art Critic and company were doing was going to affect your decision about Art?

Yes, I think I said that.

Sir, do you recall ever having seen - -

No.

- - any part of this exhibit before? I'm sorry?

No.

And my question will be the same for this exhibit.

I may have seen this.

Do you recall discussing it with Gallery Owner?

No.

Do you recall discussing it with anyone?

No.

I'll hand you what's been marked as evidence. I'll ask you if you recall ever having seen that before.

No.

Did you ever, on your own or through one of your employees, do any investigation as to whether or not Art Writer or Art Critic had lifted any pictures from <u>Art</u>?

No.

As you sit here today, do you have any opinion as to whether or not it is accurate to state that Art Writer and Art Critic lifted pictures from <u>Art</u>?

I have no opinion.

Handing you what's been marked as evidence, sir, I'll ask you to review it to determine if you recall ever having seen it before.

I don't remember seeing this.

I'll hand you what has been marked as evidence. Do you recall ever seeing that letter before?

I don't remember seeing this.

I'll hand you what's been marked as evidence and ask you if you recall ever having seen that before.

I don't think I saw this letter.

I've handed you a multi-page document marked as evidence. I'll ask you to review that document to determine if you've seen any portion of it before.

I don't think so.

Would you review this evidence, sir, to determine if you recall ever having seen that before?

Yes, I remember that letter.

Sir, referring your attention to the third paragraph, in the last sentence of that paragraph that reads, "Unfortunately it looks as if Art Critic and the

Artist estate were successful in scaring you away from publishing it as scheduled, another instance of how their actions have harmed me." Do you recall ever discussing with Gallery Owner whether or not Art Critic and the Artist estate had scared you away from publishing <u>Art for Kids</u>?

No.

That was your own decision, wasn't it, sir?

Yes.

Sir, the reporter is handing you what's been marked as evidence. I'll ask you to review that document to determine if you recognize the handwriting.

Yes.

Is that your handwriting?

Yes, it is.

In this note it refers to some technical reasons for delay in the launching <u>Art for Kids</u>. Do you recall what technical reasons you were referring to in that note?

I think they had to do with printing.

Does this note refresh your recollection that at one time you did consider publishing <u>Art for Kids</u>?

I've never had to be refreshed on that. I had intended to publish it at one time.

Perhaps I misunderstood. I thought you personally never had reviewed this book. Did I misunderstand that?

That's true. That doesn't mean I wasn't going to publish it.

Is it correct, then, that if you had reviewed this book, you might have pushed it along a bit more quickly?

Yes.

I'm just trying to understand. I thought the reason the book wasn't published is because you didn't pay much attention to it. Was that an incorrect understanding, or was there some other reason why the book wasn't published?

The children's book editor rejected it, and I went along with her.

Do you recall ever having seen this exhibit before, sir?

I might have seen that.

Do you recall discussing it with anyone?

No.

Sir, the reporter is handing you a multi-page document that is marked as evidence. I'll ask you to review it to determine if you recall ever having seen any part of it before.

I think I saw this.

Do you recall discussing any portion of it with anyone?

Yes.

Who do you recall discussing it with?

I don't remember.

Referring your attention to this portion of the evidence, do you have any specific recollection as to having reviewed before those pages in this exhibit?

I probably glanced at them, but I didn't do anything with them.

And why didn't you do anything with them?

Didn't see any reason to.

Is that because you thought the comments weren't accurate?

I think I threw this into the Gallery Owner file - -

Didn't think it required - -

- - to - -

You didn't think it required your attention?

Right.

Did you ask any one of your employees to do anything with it?

No.

Do you recall having seen this evidence before, sir?

Yes.

Do you recall discussing it with anyone?

Yes.

Who do you recall discussing it with?

I think I called Gallery Owner about that one.

And what do you recall discussing with her on that one?

I think there was a question about this image of "Painting #1."

Do you recall what that question was?

There was a misunderstanding about whether it could be used as a special part of <u>Contemporary Art</u>.

I'll hand you what's been marked as evidence. I'll ask you if you recall having seen that before.

Yes, I've seen that.

And directing your attention to the second paragraph, the sentence that appears to read, "I'm going for a felony conviction for slander and trade interference," do you recall ever discussing that language with Gallery Owner?

No.

Do you recall ever discussing it with anyone else?

No.

Do you recall ever discussing with anyone any assertions by Gallery Owner that Art Writer or Art Critic had committed a crime?

I discussed with Gallery Owner her feeling that she had been wronged.

All right, sir. The specific question is did you ever discuss with anyone her assertion that Art Critic and Art Writer had committed a crime, a felony?

I don't remember the word "felony" being used.

Do you remember the word "crime" being used?

No.

I'll hand you what's been marked as evidence, and I'll ask you if you recall ever having seen this document before.

Yes.

Is that your handwriting?

Yes.

What does it refer to?

An auction of an Artist painting.

Do you recall what painting?

Yes.

Which painting?

"Painting #2."

I'll ask you to review what's been marked as evidence and ask you if you've ever seen that before.

Yes, I've seen this letter.

Do you recall discussing it with anyone?

No.

Did you make any response to this letter?

No, I didn't.

Did this letter have any effect on your business relationship with Gallery Owner?

None.

Do you recall ever stating that you believed Gallery Owner was possessed by Artist's ghost?

I don't remember saying that.

Do you recall if Gallery Owner ever approached you about a possible investment in the artwork "Painting #3"?

Yes.

Did you make that investment?

No.

Why not?

I didn't really want to own any Artist paintings.

Do you recall stating after this investment opportunity arose that you felt fortunate that you hadn't invested in the painting?

No.

I'll pass the witness.

Any objection to taking a short break?

That's fine.

(Brief recess.)

Good afternoon, Publisher. I'm Gallery Owner's lawyer and I represent Gallery Owner in this case. Nice to meet you.

Thank you. Nice to meet you.

I think you've answered my first question, which is, do you recognize this evidence?

Yes.

This exhibit, for the record, is a two-page document. And if you could, let's start with the second page of it. And since you're probably getting tired, why don't I read what I think is your writing on the page, and you interrupt me and tell me if I've read anything incorrectly, okay?

Thank you, Counsel.

"Dear Gallery Owner, please" - - I can't read the second word.

"Please and"?

I'm sorry.

What word are you - -

The second word after "please." Well, let me try. "Please and consider the insertion that I plan to put in <u>Art</u>, second edition. This idea arose out of my meetings and discussions with Art Writer and Art Critic. Of course, they tried everything, including a lawsuit to stop the second edition, and the purpose and intent is to embarrass them in the trade. I trust you will see the irony of this and will agree that it will have the desired effect. RSVP, Publisher." Did I read that part correctly?

Yes, you did.

And on the first page of the exhibit, in the center there is a figure, an image. Can you just describe for me what that figure is in the center?

It's an Artist ink drawing of thieves, I think.

And underneath that image it says, "The publisher wishes to thank the

Artist Family Trust, Art Writer, Art Critic, and American Art, Incorporated for their friendship, interest and encouragement." Is that the proposed insert that you were referring to in your note to Gallery Owner?

Yes.

My question is, when you wrote this note to Gallery Owner - - let me start with this. Do you recall when you wrote this note to Gallery Owner?

Probably early summer. I'm speculating. I don't know exactly.

At the time you wrote this, did you believe that Art Writer and Art Critic tried everything, including a lawsuit, to stop <u>Art</u>, second edition?

That's what I wrote.

At the time you wrote this, did you believe that Art Writer and Art Critic tried to stop <u>Art</u>, second edition?

Yes, they did.

Did you believe that they brought a lawsuit against Publishing House as part of their effort to try to stop <u>Art</u>, second edition?

I guess they did.

Was that what you believed when you wrote this letter?

Yeah.

Do you still believe that?

After today, yes.

Is there anything in particular about what's happening today which has confirmed that belief in your mind?

I think one of the lawsuits names Publishing House.

Is that the New England lawsuit?

I don't know which one.

Do you recall that one lawsuit was filed against Publishing House in a New England Court in the fall of last year?

Yes.

Let me ask again, though, is there anything specific about anything that's happened today or any of the documents you've seen today, or any memories that have been refreshed by today's deposition which has confirmed in your mind your belief that Art Critic and Art Writer brought a lawsuit against Publishing House for the purpose of stopping Art?

I don't know.

And you didn't use this insert in <u>Art</u>, second edition, did you?

One copy.

Do you know where that copy is?

Yes.

Where is it?

In my office.

Has that copy been shown to anybody else, outside of Publishing House?

No.

Can you think of anything else besides bringing a lawsuit against Publishing House that you believe Art Writer and Art Critic have done to try and stop <u>Art</u>, second edition?

They visited my office twice.

And in those, during those visits did they request that you not publish <u>Art</u>, second edition?

Yes.

Did they demand that you not publish <u>Art</u>, second edition?

Persuade, I think, would be a better word. Or tried to.

How did they attempt to persuade you?

They tried to point out errors in the book.

Did they also threaten to sue Publishing House if it were to proceed with
<u>Art</u>, second edition?

I don't remember.

Now, as a result of Publishing House being sued by Art Writer, Art
Critic and the Artist Family Trust, isn't it true that Publishing House
has informed Gallery Owner that it's going to be withholding any
royalties that are owing to her in order to use those royalties to defer
Publishing House's legal expenses?

Lacks foundation. And Vague. Compound.

You may answer if you understand the question.

The boilerplate on our contract would determine what would happen in
a situation like that.

Do you know whether or not Publishing House is currently withholding
royalties from Gallery Owner on the grounds that those royalties are to
be used to defer Publishing House's legal expenses in connection - -

I don't know.

You don't know?

No.

Who at your company would know about that?

General Manager.

Do you know how royalties are calculated with respect to <u>Art</u> or <u>Art</u>, second edition?

Yes.

How are they calculated?

Very carefully.

Sir, isn't it that 8.5 percent of list price goes to Gallery Owner with respect to those publications?

I think it's 8.5 percent of net sales.

I'll tell my client to bear in mind that you only testify to what you absolutely know about.

Okay.

Is it your recollection that Publishing House pays, or is supposed to pay Gallery Owner 8.5 percent of net sales of all <u>Art</u> and <u>Art</u>, second edition books sold?

The contract that I remember signing for <u>Art</u>, I believe gave her 8.5 percent of the net sales. I don't remember the <u>Art</u>, second edition contract.

Do you remember that the contract for <u>Art</u> was cancelled at one point?

No.

Do you recall contacting Gallery Owner and informing her that because you had discovered that she was going to be publishing a book on Artist with Publishing Company, that Publishing House would have to consider the contract for <u>Art</u> to be null and void?

I do remember that.

What do you remember about that?

That we informed her that she shouldn't do both. And we were willing to go ahead if she would not do the other one. She agreed to not do the other one, so we pushed forward with <u>Art</u>.

Why did you not want to publish <u>Art</u> - - let me start that question over. What was it about Gallery Owner's plans to publish books with Publishing Company that concerned you and made you contact her and ask her to choose your book or the Publishing Company book?

I thought they would compete with each other in such a way that it would be unfavorable to the main, the large book.

The large book is <u>Art</u>?

Yeah.

And what led you to believe that the books would compete with each other?

Just my opinion. But primarily it was in violation of her contract with me.

Let's take a look at - - let's mark this. Publisher, is this evidence a letter that you wrote to Gallery Owner in the summer of four years ago?

Looks like it.

Does this refresh your recollection that you requested, that you informed Gallery Owner that the contract for <u>Art</u> was no longer in effect? And I'll just direct your attention to the first sentence in the fourth paragraph.

Which sentence are you referring to?

"Thus, we need to start over on a new contract, if we can."

All right. I remember that now.

So at that point in time you considered the contract for <u>Art</u> to be cancelled, is that correct?

I don't remember what the discussion was with Gallery Owner at that particular time.

Do you know if a new contract for <u>Art</u> was ever signed?

Yes.

There was a contract signed, or there wasn't?

There was a contract signed by both parties, I believe. And it was the same as the first one.

Do you know if Publishing House has a copy of that contract in its files?

I understand that we can't find a signed copy.

Let's take a look at this evidence.

Is there a question pending?

No, I'm just looking for an exhibit. Here it is. Take a look at this evidence. As of the beginning of this year, you were at least discussing with Art Writer and Art Critic the possibility of publishing a book with them in respect to Artist, isn't that correct?

Yes and no.

Explain the yes and explain the no.

I didn't expect to publish a book with them, but I wanted to find out what they were up to.

They were planning, is it your understanding that they were planning to publish a book on Artist that would compete in the marketplace with Art, second edition?

If they were, Art would give them a lot of trouble.

Now, in light of what we saw before with respect to what happened with the Publishing Company book and your feelings on how the Publishing Company book would have competed with Art, let me ask you this question. Would you have published a book with Art Critic and Art Writer in the beginning of this year and also published Art, second edition?

Lacks foundation - -

Also - -

- - based on the testimony of the witness.

Also calls for speculation.

Let me rephrase it. Did you have any plans, to your recollection, in the beginning of the year of publishing a book on Artist with Art Critic and

Art Writer?

No.

Is there any reason why you didn't have those types of plans?

There isn't room for another expensive Artist book.

You would have had to choose between one or the other, isn't that true?

Objection. Calls for speculation.

It really does.

In the beginning of the year, without disclosing to me anything you might have discussed with your counsel, were you attempting to settle the New England action with Art Critic and Art Writer?

No.

And your second sentence on this exhibit says, "Is there more than a hint of some hidden agenda to which I am not privy?" Can you please explain what you were referring to there, when you wrote that sentence?

Yes. The hidden agenda was, in my mind, a book that they were contemplating.

Is it fair to say that you believed that their hidden agenda was to stop or hinder Art so that they could bring their book - -

Objection. Mischaracterizes the witness's testimony.

That is what I was thinking, though.

That is what you were thinking when you wrote that sentence?

Yes, that's right.

And the first sentence refers to friendly and good-natured talks that you've had with Art Critic and Art Writer. And you've already testified about those a little bit. My question to you is, has Art Critic or Art Writer, have either of them ever had anything friendly or good-natured to say about Gallery Owner?

No.

Would it be fair to say that - - well, why don't you, if you could, please tell me to the best of your recollection what Art Critic or Art Writer has had to say about Gallery Owner.

They were unfriendly competitors of hers.

And they were the first people to tell you that Gallery Owner had had a felony conviction, isn't that true?

Yes.

Do you remember anything they said on that general subject?

Just that it had occurred.

And they told you that Gallery Owner is, has been selling fake works of art, isn't that true?

Yes they did.

But they have never given you any facts to support that, have they?

Nothing credible.

What do you recall, what information do you recall has been provided to you by either Art Critic, Art Writer, or anyone associated with them, with respect to the allegation that Gallery Owner has sold fake Artist works of art?

I can't think of anything that we haven't seen today.

So are you referring to the correspondence and so forth where they have made those allegations?

Yes.

Did you ever state to either Art Critic or Art Writer that Publishing House would not reprint <u>Art</u>?

No.

You never stated that?

I don't think so.

So if someone were to say that you had said that, they would be mistaken, is that correct?

The book was out of print. There was demand for it. I hadn't made up my mind whether to do it again.

What factors were you considering in your mind when you were trying to decide whether or not to publish <u>Art</u>, second edition?

Objection. Asked and answered very capably under earlier examination.

Do you recall any other factors you were considering?

Visibility in the marketplace.

Anything else?

No.

Have you ever been contacted by Art Professor or anyone representing Art Professor?

No.

Let's mark this as the next one. Publisher, this exhibit is a three-page document that appears to be a letter from Art Scholar to Art Collector. Have you seen this document before?

Well, I don't remember it offhand.

Just a yes or no will suffice.

Counsel, I think - -

I haven't finished reading this.

I think you and I need to consult about this. We haven't consulted about this evidence, and it's marked highly confidential.

I'm sorry. Do you have any objection to me showing it to the witness?

Well, it's a little late. I guess it's a confidential document for purposes of this deposition. I'll permit that.

I apologize for that mix-up.

Is there a question pending?

Well, I asked if he had ever seen it. I can't recall whether there was an answer. Have you ever seen it?

I don't remember.

Did you ever state that no editing had been done for the content of <u>Art</u>?

Objection. Vague as to time.

I think that I said there was no editing as to content, but there was thorough editing as to form.

Did you ever admit that <u>Art</u> contained plagiarism?

Objection. Vague as to form, time. It's really hard to give any dimension to that. You can answer the question to the extent that you are able.

Well, I was never really aware of any plagiarism.

Did anyone ever provide you with any facts that would support the allegation that there was plagiarism in <u>Art</u>?

There were allegations of plagiarism, but I did not take them seriously.

Were there any facts provided to you to support those allegations by anyone?

By plagiarism, what do you mean? Illegal plagiarism, or quotes that are too long?

Any type of plagiarism. Let me ask you another question. This is what I'm trying to get at. We have seen several documents over the course of today's deposition where there have been allegations and letters sent to you saying that there is plagiarism in <u>Art</u>.

Uh-huh.

All I'm trying to ask is, other than just the allegations of plagiarism, has anyone ever provided you with facts to support those allegations, that you recall?

Nothing that I took seriously.

Do you have anything specific that we saw today which would tend to support the allegation of plagiarism?

This exhibit.

Objection.

Why don't we take a look at it. Take a quick look at this evidence. Tell me if there is anything in that document which you believe is a fact which supports an allegation of plagiarism in <u>Art</u>.

Counsel, this exhibit is a ten-page document. Do you really intend for us to sit here and carefully go through this?

Well, no. I just wanted to clear up the - -

I think I can answer it.

Do you still have my question in mind, or do you want it read back?

I didn't consider this anything like proof of plagiarism.

Have you ever been shown anything else other than what's in this evidence that would tend to substantiate the allegations of plagiarism that had been made with respect to <u>Art</u>?

Anything that is in exhibits today, no.

Okay. This evidence is a two-page document. It's a letter from Art Collector to Art Scholar, from late winter of last year. Do you recognize this document, Publisher?

I may have seen this, I don't know.

On the second page, the second full paragraph, there is a reference to "the complete disauthenticating documentation will be turned over to you at an appropriate time and at an appropriate venue." Did anyone ever turn over to you documentation which would tend to demonstrate that any of the works depicted in <u>Art</u> were not authentic Artist works?

Nothing that we haven't seen today.

Okay. The last paragraph says, "This case seems to be nothing more than frivolous, malicious prosecution of Publishing House by your clients." Did you agree in the winter of last year that the action filed against you by Art Critic and Art Writer was a frivolous and malicious prosecution of Publishing House?

Yes, I did.

Did you ever receive any affidavits or information from any art experts which indicated that any of the paintings which are depicted in <u>Art</u> were not authentic Artist paintings?

No.

Do you still have this evidence in front of you?

Which one is it, exhibit what?

Starts out, it's summer of two years ago. Take a look at the second page of that if you could.

Second page?

Yes. That's a memo from Art Writer to Managing Editor. Who is Managing Editor?

One of my employees.

It says, "Managing Editor, I really enjoyed talking to you this afternoon, and in the interest of continuing our" quote, "off-the-record discussions," close quote, "send herewith the letters which we just received." Did Managing Editor ever discuss with you any off-the-record discussions that she had had with Art Writer?

Yes.

What did she tell you about those?

I don't remember.

Did they concern Gallery Owner?

Yes.

Do you remember just generally what the topic was, with respect to Gallery Owner?

Negative things.

And then the next sentence says, "Realizing that our fax number and answer back code are emblazoned above, I would like to kindly request that you expunge them from all sheets before showing them to anybody. Thank you for your openness and frank talk." Do you remember discussing with Managing Editor or anyone else Art Writer's request that he expunge his fax number from anything that he faxed to Publishing House?

No.

Did you ever discuss that topic with Art Writer?

No.

Did he ever ask you to keep any discussions with you with respect to Gallery Owner or <u>Art</u> confidential or off the record?

No.

When Art Writer and Art Critic's Lawyer was asking you questions earlier today about the text of <u>Art</u>, you referred to it as lightweight, I believe. Do you recall that testimony?

Yes.

What did you mean by the word "lightweight"?

It generally didn't get first-rate reviews. It got middling reviews, the text.

Do you recall anyone specific that gave it not-great reviews? Or that criticized the text?

The reviewers generally loved the book, the pictures, and gave middling reviews to the text.

Do you have any opinion with respect to whether or not the existence of the dispute between Gallery Owner and Art Critic and Art Writer and the Artist Family Trust is widely known in the art industry?

Lacks foundation. Calls for speculation.

I'm asking for an opinion.

Same objection.

I don't have contact in the art world that would give any worth to my answer on that. So I don't know.

What about the publishing world?

Same objections.

I don't know of any problem in the publishing world.

Do you have any opinion as to whether or not the dispute that brings us together today has had any effect on the sales of any of the books that Publishing House has published with Gallery Owner?

Vague. Lacks foundation.

I don't know.

Okay. Do you believe that it's helped sales?

Same objections.

I don't know.

The question of whether or not the book, the second edition of the book would sell certainly factored into your decision whether or not to publish Art, isn't that true?

Say that again?

The issue of whether or not the book would sell in the market certainly

factored into your decision as to whether or not to go forward with the
second edition?

Yes.

Did you consider whether or not this dispute that brings us together
today would have any impact on the sales of the second edition?

No.

Okay. Anybody at Publishing House ever raise that concern with you?

No.

Let's take a look at this evidence if you would. That is the affidavit of Art
Writer and Art Critic, which is in front of you. The first paragraph of
this affidavit says, "Based upon a telephone conversation which I, Art
Critic, had with Publisher during the last week of last year, the
publication entitled <u>Art</u>, a book written by Gallery Owner and published
by Publishing House, had sold tens of thousands of copies and thousands
of limited edition copies throughout the United States and overseas."
That is my question. Do you know how many copies of that book had
been sold?

No.

Okay. Let's look at paragraph 4 on the next page. It says, "The beginning
of each chapter of <u>Art</u> contains an image of an Artist work entitled
'Drawing #1.' This image was reproduced utilizing a transparency which

is the property of Art Critic without having obtained her permission for its use." My question to you is, has anyone ever provided you with any facts to support the allegation that the transparencies of "Drawing #1" in <u>Art</u> are the property of Art Critic and were obtained without her permission?

No.

Skipping down to paragraph 5. "In late summer of two years ago, I, Art Writer, talked with Managing Editor again and asked that they not publish <u>Art</u>, second edition, as we had just seen an announcement for the same. It is now our belief that they may have done so and not changed the edition number. This belief is based upon Art Scholar, a noted Artist authority, stating that the bookstores had sold out, and now it is back on the shelf." My question to you is, did you republish <u>Art</u> and not change the edition number?

No.

Do you know who Art Scholar is?

No.

Paragraph 6 refers to a conversation between, an alleged conversation between yourself and Art Writer in early fall of two years ago. And in the last sentence of that paragraph says, "He," which I believe is referring to you, "also informed me that I was not the first person who had contacted him regarding deficiencies of <u>Art</u>." My question is, is it true that Art Writer was not the first person who had contacted you regarding deficiencies in <u>Art</u>?

I don't remember anybody else.

Do you recall ever stating to Art Writer that he was not the first person that had contacted you with respect to deficiencies in <u>Art</u>?

I don't really have a recollection of that.

And I apologize if I've already asked this question, but bear with me. Do you recall anyone else, other than Art Writer and Art Critic, contacting you with respect to alleged deficiencies in <u>Art</u>? And I'll add, or attorneys representing them. Has anyone other than Art Critic, Art Writer, or attorneys representing them ever contacted you with respect to alleged deficiencies in <u>Art</u>?

No.

Paragraph 8 refers to a conversation that allegedly occurred between you and Art Writer. In the second sentence it states, "I, Art Writer, telephoned Publisher to inquire about the second edition and was informed that the poor showing of the first edition would likely result in there being no second edition." My question is, did you inform Art Writer that because of the poor showing of the first edition that there would likely be no second edition?

I don't think so.

Do you have any recollection of saying that - -

No.

- - to Art Writer? Do you recall saying that to him at any time?

No.

This exhibit is the next in order. That is a two-page document on the letterhead of the law firm of Art Lawyer, and it's dated winter of last year. Publisher, do you recall ever seeing this document before?

I'm not sure that I did. I might have.

And again, did anyone ever provide you with any information to support the allegation that the works of art listed in this exhibit were fake works of art?

Nothing that was interesting enough for me to remember.

So are you stating, then, that you don't recollect anything that was communicated to you with respect to the allegations that these were fakes?

Right.

Now let's look at this evidence. It's dated the beginning of this year, a letter from Publishing House Lawyer to Art Lawyer. Did you ever see this document before?

Might have.

The last full paragraph on the first page says, "We demand that you provide us with either the names and the addresses of the experts to whom the affidavit refers, or sworn declarations of such experts setting forth their qualifications and the basis of their opinions, within ten days of this letter." And again, my question is, do you recall whether or not Art Writer or Art Critic or any attorney representing them ever provided you with any affidavits or sworn declarations of fine art experts which would tend to substantiate the claims that works of art in <u>Art</u> were not authentic Artist works?

I don't remember any.

Second page of the letter, your lawyer says in her second sentence, "It is improper for the plaintiffs to use their lawsuit to attempt to stifle our client's First Amendment right as a publisher." My question to you is, do you agree with your lawyer's statement that the lawsuit that was filed against Publishing House by Art Critic and Art Writer was an attempt to stifle the First Amendment rights of your company?

No.

Did you review this letter before your lawyer sent it out?

I don't think so.

Did you believe there was any merit to the lawsuit that was filed against Publishing House by Art Critic and Art Writer?

No, I didn't.

Okay. I think that's all I have.

I have just a few questions to follow up on what counsel asked you.

He gets a rebuttal.

(Further Examination By Art Writer and Art Critic's Lawyer.)

Sir, who has seen the single copy of <u>Art</u>, second edition that's in your office bearing the logo that appears on the first page of this exhibit, referring to the Artist Family Trust, Art Writer and Art Critic?

I intended to send one copy of the book with this in it to Art Writer and Art Critic. Sort of a joke.

You haven't done it yet?

I haven't done it. I will not do it.

Who has seen it, though?

Just me.

No other employees of your company?

No. No.

On the second page of that same exhibit, the handwritten notes in the upper left-hand corner, are those your notes numbered 1, 3 and 4, in the upper left-hand corner?

Yes.

Note 3, I'll attempt to read it. Correct me if you think I'm reading it wrong. "We stand by you through legal problems that we strongly advised against." Is that a correct reading, sir?

Yes.

Other than what you've already testified to here today, do you have anything to add to the topic of you having strongly advised against any legal actions by Gallery Owner? We already covered that topic?

We covered it.

You said, sir, that when you, in the beginning of this year were discussing the possibility of doing a book with Art Writer and/or Art Critic, that you didn't really expect to work with them, but you wanted to know what they were up to. Is that an accurate recitation of what your mindset was at the time you were talking to them in the beginning of the year?

I was going on what my lawyer would call a fishing expedition.

What were you fishing for?

Information.

What kind of information?

What was in the wind.

Such as?

New books, fish, projects.

Did you tell Art Writer or Art Critic that you were engaging in a fishing expedition and weren't seriously interested in working with them?

Fishing expeditions sometimes get serious, so I wouldn't have any business saying anything like that.

Is it your testimony now, then, that in the beginning of the year there was the possibility of doing a book with Art Writer and Art Critic?

When you go fishing, you never know what you're going to catch.

So that possibility is one possible outcome of this fishing expedition?

You never know.

I'm asking you, sir.

Like I say, you never know.

Who first told you that Gallery Owner was involved in the sale of fakes?

Objection. That assumes that's a fact.

Well, he's testified that he was told that.

I don't remember.

All right. Do you remember if anyone other than Art Writer has ever discussed with you the possibility that Gallery Owner was involved in the sale of fakes?

No, I don't think so.

Do you remember having a discussion with Art Writer on that topic?

That's the likely source.

But you don't remember, do you?

No.

And you don't remember having any discussion with Art Critic about sales of fakes by Gallery Owner either, do you?

No.

You don't remember any such conversations, is that correct?

I've already said the he was the likely source.

Art Writer was the likely source?

Or Art Critic.

Or Art Critic?

Or Art Critic and Art Writer.

But as you sit here today you don't remember a discussion with either one of them where they told you that Gallery Owner was involved in the sale of fakes, do you?

A specific discussion, a date and time, no.

As you sit here today, do you definitely recall that it was one of them that told you that Gallery Owner was involved in the sale of fakes?

Only by elimination. I never discussed this with anyone else.

As far as you remember.

I'm pretty sure that I never discussed possible fakes of her gallery with anybody else.

Have you ever been in, contacted by any law enforcement officials on that topic?

Oh, no.

If we could get that evidence.

Again?

That's the one that was just kindly re-filed for us. Okay. Sir, in this exhibit, the third page of the exhibit, did you ever check any of the citations on that page to Art Professor's book?

No.

So as you sit here today you don't know whether there was any direct copying from Art Professor's book to Gallery Owner's <u>Art</u>, do you?

No.

Directing your attention to this evidence, paragraph 4. Do you have that exhibit in front of you, sir?

Yes.

Could you turn to the second page, paragraph 4. My question is this, do you know where the transparency was obtained that was used - -

No.

- - let me finish the question, sir. Thank you for your answer, but let me finish the question. Do you know where the transparency was obtained for the work "Drawing #1" that was used in <u>Art</u>?

No.

Thank you, sir. Did anyone ever tell you where it was obtained?

No.

One last question on this evidence. Who selected the image that appears in the center of the first page of this exhibit?

I don't really know.

It wasn't you?

It wasn't me.

Was it one of your employees?

I really don't know.

Who typeset or otherwise prepared this legend in the middle of the page that includes this image and the good wishes of the publisher are to the Artist Family Trust, Art Writer and Art Critic. Who physically prepared this?

Designer.

Was anyone else involved in the preparation of this?

Only a typesetter that wouldn't know what he was reading.

This is just a typesetter that worked for your company?

Yes.

Did Designer do this on his own initiative, or was it at your request?

At my request.

Other than yourself and Designer, was anyone else involved in the preparation of this logo and the language that appears just beneath it?

No.

As you sit here today, are you aware of any statements or actions by Art Writer that in any way restricted Gallery Owner's ability to be published by yourself or any other publisher with regard to any work relating to Artist?

I can only speak about my own company.

All right. As to your own company?

I didn't feel prevented from having my First Amendment rights.

You felt like you could do what you wanted to, despite what Art Writer said and did, is that correct?

That's correct.

Is your answer the same for Art Critic?

Yes.

And is your answer the same for the Artist Family Trust?

That's true.

Answer the same for American Art, Incorporated?

Yes.

Answer the same for Publishing Company?

Yes.

Is your answer the same for Artist's Daughter?

Uh-huh.

Is your answer the same for Publishing Corporation?

Yes.

Is your answer the same for Art Organization?

Yes.

I have no further questions of this witness.

Made in the USA
Monee, IL
07 July 2026

56552032R00095